IT'S TIME TO EAT SAUSAGE SPAGHETTI

It's Time to Eat SAUSAGE SPAGHETTI

Walter the Educator

Silent King Books
A WhichHead Entertainment Imprint

Copyright © 2024 by Walter the Educator

All rights reserved. No part of this book may be reproduced in any manner whatsoever without written per- mission except in the case of brief quotations embodied in critical articles and reviews.

First Printing, 2024

Disclaimer

This book is a literary work; the story is not about specific persons, locations, situations, and/or circumstances unless mentioned in a historical context. Any resemblance to real persons, locations, situations, and/or circumstances is coincidental. This book is for entertainment and informational purposes only. The author and publisher offer this information without warranties expressed or implied. No matter the grounds, neither the author nor the publisher will be accountable for any losses, injuries, or other damages caused by the reader's use of this book. The use of this book acknowledges an understanding and acceptance of this disclaimer.

It's Time to Eat SAUSAGE SPAGHETTI is a collectible early learning book by Walter the Educator suitable for all ages belonging to Walter the Educator's Time to Eat Book Series. Collect more books at WaltertheEducator.com

USE THE EXTRA SPACE TO TAKE NOTES AND DOCUMENT YOUR MEMORIES

SAUSAGE SPAGHETTI

Oh, what's that smell that fills the air?

It's Time to Eat

Sausage Spaghetti

It's coming from the kitchen, I declare!

Sausage spaghetti, piping hot,

Dinner's ready, what a spot!

The noodles twirl on the fork so fine,

They wiggle and dance, a tasty sign.

With sausage bits so round and small,

I can't wait to eat them all!

The sauce is red like a sunset sky,

Tomatoes and spices piled high.

A sprinkle of cheese makes it complete,

Oh, sausage spaghetti, you can't be beat!

Mama says, "Take a little bite,

Chew it slowly, don't rush tonight."

It's warm and cozy, a hug on my plate,

Sausage spaghetti is always first-rate!

It's Time to Eat
Sausage Spaghetti

Twirl and twirl, the noodles go,

Round and round, like a spinning show.

I slurp one up, what a slippery treat,

Eating spaghetti is such a feat!

The sausages pop with a yummy sound,

Each little bite is a flavor profound.

Mixing the sauce and noodles so sweet,

Every spoonful's a savory beat.

Daddy laughs as I make a mess,

Sauce on my chin and all the rest.

But he wipes it clean with a loving smile,

Sausage spaghetti is worth the while!

The bowl gets empty; my tummy's full,

That sausage spaghetti sure was cool!

"More, please!" I say, with a happy grin,

It's Time to Eat Sausage Spaghetti

Can we have this again and again?

So remember, friends, when it's time to eat,

Sausage spaghetti's a tasty treat.

Grab your fork, don't be late,

A delicious dinner is on your plate!

The family gathers, the laughter flows,

A meal like this, everybody knows,

Is more than food, it's love to share,

It's Time to Eat
Sausage Spaghetti

Sausage spaghetti shows we care!

ABOUT THE CREATOR

Walter the Educator is one of the pseudonyms for Walter Anderson. Formally educated in Chemistry, Business, and Education, he is an educator, an author, a diverse entrepreneur, and he is the son of a disabled war veteran. "Walter the Educator" shares his time between educating and creating. He holds interests and owns several creative projects that entertain, enlighten, enhance, and educate, hoping to inspire and motivate you. Follow, find new works, and stay up to date with Walter the Educator™ at WaltertheEducator.com

www.ingramcontent.com/pod-product-compliance
Lightning Source LLC
LaVergne TN
LVHW052014060526
838201LV00059B/4036